MEN-AT-ARMS SERIES

EDITOR: MARTIN WINDRO
ALBAN BOOK SERVICES

Napoleon's German Allies (1)

Westfalia and Kleve-Berg

Text by OTTO VON PIVKA

Colour plates by MICHAEL ROFFE

OSPREY PUBLISHING LIMITED

Published in 1975 by
Osprey Publishing Ltd, 137 Southampton Street,
Reading, Berkshire
© Copyright 1975 Osprey Publishing Ltd

The author's thanks are due to the following, who were of
assistance to him in the preparation of this book:
the authorities in the Braunschweigische Landesmuseum,
the members of the Gesellschaft für Heereskunde in
Berlin and Hamburg, the members of the Bergische Geschichtliche
Verein and Rosie.

paper edition ISBN 0 85045 211 2
cased edition ISBN 0 85045 234 1

Printed in Great Britain by
Jarrold & Sons Ltd, Norwich

Napoleon's German Allies

THE KINGDOM OF WESTFALIA AND THE GRAND DUCHY OF KLEVE-BERG

The emergence of revolutionary France as an aggressive and capable military power at the end of the eighteenth century, caused the collapse of the Holy Roman Empire (a loose coalition of German states, usually under Austria's leadership). Austria's defeat at the Battle of Hohenlinden, on 3 December 1800, created a power vacuum in the area now known as Germany, and Napoleon lost little time in transforming this neutralized zone into a pro-French *cordon sanitaire* between France and her traditional eastern enemies – Austria, Prussia, and Russia. In 1803 France occupied Hanover; in 1805 France and Bavaria defeated Austria and Russia at Ulm (17 October 1805) and Austerlitz (2 December 1805). As a final step in the creation of the *cordon sanitaire*, Napoleon formed a Confederation of the Rhine (Der Rheinbund) which was eventually to include the following states: France; the kingdoms of Bavaria, Saxony, Westfalia and Württemberg; the duchies of Kleve-Berg, Warsaw, Baden, Hessen-Darmstadt Oldenburg; and the principalities of Sachsen-Weimar, Sachsen-Coburg Saalfeld, Sachsen-Gotha-Altenburg, Sachsen-Hildburghausen, Sachsen-Meiningen, Schwarzburg-Rudolstadt, Schwarzburg-Sondershausen, the five Houses of Reuss, Mecklenburg-Schwerin, Mecklenburg-Strelitz, Waldeck, Anhalt-Bernburg, Anhalt-Dessau, Anhalt-Köthen, Hohenzollern-Hechingen, Hohenzollern-Sigmaringen, Lippe-Detmold, Schaumburg-Lippe, Isenburg, Leyen,

Lichtenstein, Würzburg; and the city states of Frankfurt and Erfurt.

Confusing as this list may appear, it greatly simplified the situation which had existed prior to 1800, when there had been an even greater number of tiny, independent states within Germany.

Grand Duchy of Kleve-Berg

Napoleon decreed the formation of the Grand Duchy of Berg on 14 November 1808. This was a rearrangement of territory subsequent to the donation of Hanover to Prussia by France on 15 December 1805. In exchange, Prussia gave up Kleve and the fortress of Wesel. Furthermore, Bavaria released Ansbach and the Herzogtum Berg to Napoleon, who rewarded the Bavarian Prince Elector with Austrian lands and the title of King. Napoleon united Kleve and Berg, nominated Düsseldorf to be the capital, and gave the throne

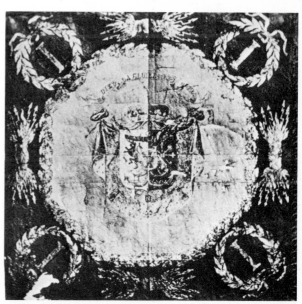

Grand Duchy of Berg: flag design 1807. The colours are red and white, with gold embroidery

Decree concerning the number of conscripts to be raised in the Rhineland when the area was under French control

to his brother-in-law, Joachim Murat, later King of Naples. After the Peace of Tilsit the grand duchy received the duchies of Mark and Dortmund from Prussia.

The decree of 14 November 1808 reads thus:

AT THE IMPERIAL HEADQUARTERS IN BURGOS,
14 NOVEMBER 1808

Napoleon, Emperor of the French, King of Italy, Protector of the Rheinbund, Grand-Duke of Kleve and Berg, etc.

On the submission of our minister of the Grand Duchy of Berg and the State senate, we have decided as follows:

First Article

The Grand Duchy of Berg will be divided into four departments.

1 The Department of the Rhine

It will consist of the old Duchy of Berg with the exception of Windeck and part of Blankenberg; of the lands vacated by the Duke of Nassau Vilich; Wolkenburg; Deutz; of the Baronies of Broich, Styrum and Hardenberg of the Herrlichkeiten; Elten; Essen; and Werden; and of those parts of the Duchy of Kleve which lie on the right bank of the Rhine with the exception of the French-ruled town of Wesel and the area belonging to it, and the Districts of Huissen, Sevenaer and Malburgen which will go to Holland.

  Population: 322,284 souls

  Capital: Düsseldorf

  It will be divided into four districts: Düsseldorf, Elberfeld, Mülheim, Essen.

2 The Department of the Sieg

It consists of Windeck and part of Blankenberg; of the Baronies of Homburg, Gimborn-Neustadt and Wildenburg; of the Principalities of Siegen and Dillenburg, in the latter case with the exception of Burbach which will go to Nassau; of the barony of Beilstein and the Principality of Hadamar; of those parts of the Herrschaften of Schadeck and Runkel which lie on the right bank of the Lahn; and of the Herrschaft of Westerburg.

  Population: 133,070 souls

  Capital: Dillenburg

  It will be divided into two districts: Siegen, Dillenburg.

3 The Department of the Ruhr

It consists of the Counties of Mark, Dortmund and Limburg, part of the Principality of Münster; the Herrschaft Rheda and of the town of Lippstadt and its area.

  Population: 212,602 souls

  Capital: Dortmund

  It will be divided into three districts: Dortmund, Hagen, Hamm.

4 The Department of the Ems

It consists of the greater part of the Principality of Münster; of the Counties of Horstmar and Rheina-Wolbeck; of the Counties of Steinfurt and Bentheim; and of the Counties of Lingen and Tecklenburg.

  Population: 210,201 souls

  Capital: Münster

  It will be divided into three districts: Münster, Coesfeld, Lingen.

Article 2
The cantons and parishes of which the districts will consist, and the borders of the Departments, are drawn on the attached map.

Article 3
Our ministers in the Grand Duchy of Berg are charged with the execution of this decree.

Signed: Napoleon

By this time the grand duchy had a new ruler, Napoleon himself. Murat had left Berg under a decree of 15 July 1808 to become King of Naples. A decree of 3 March 1809 gave Berg to the young nephew of the Emperor, Louis, the eldest son of the King of Holland. Napoleon became Regent until the boy should become of age. By a Senate decree of 13 December 1810, the grand duchy lost the north-east part of the Principality of Münster, and all parts of the Department of the Ems. These lost provinces became French Departments. In 1811, however, it was increased again by the addition of the Duchy of Recklinghausen and part of the Amt of Dülmen. Berg remained so until its dissolution in 1813.

Flag of the 5th Westfalian Line Infantry being paraded in Hamburg in 1809: a print. (C. Suhr)

Kingdom of Westfalia

The process of formation of the kingdom of Westfalia was somewhat simpler. This state was born at the Peace of Tilsit, and was a gift by Napoleon to Jerome, his favourite brother. An imperial decree of 15 November 1807 from Fontainebleau announced the constitution of the new state. King Jerome decreed the formation of the Departments of this kingdom in a decree from Kassel, its capital, on 24 December 1807:

In the palace of Kassel 24 December 1807
We Hieronymus Napoleon, etc
order that the Kingdom of Westfalia shall be
divided into eight Departments:

1 The Department of the Elbe
It will consist of the greatest part of the Duchy of Magdeburg; of the Duchy of Barby; of the Aemtern of Gommersch, which has come from Saxony; of the Alt Mark; of the Brunswick Amt Calvorde and the Amt Weserlingen.

Population: 253,210 people
Capital: Magdeburg
It will be divided into four districts: Magdeburg, Neupaldensleben, Stendal, Salzwedel.

2 The Department of Fulda
It will consist of a part of Nieder-Hessen; the state [*Land*] of Paderborn; of the areas of Corvey; of the Amt Reckenburg; of the County of Rietberg Kaunitz; and the Amt of Munden.
Population: 239,502 people
Capital: Kassel
It will be divided into three districts: Kassel, Höxter, Paderborn.

3 The Department of the Harz
It will consist of the Principality of Eichsfeld; of the County of Hohenstein; of part of the Principality of Grubenhagen; of the area of Walkenried; of part of the *Land* of Blankenburg; of part of

Trooper of 1st Westfalian Kürassiers in the first uniform of that regiment: a contemporary plate. (C. Suhr)

Hildesheim; the town and area of Goslar; some of the villages of the *Land* of Magdeburg; and Halberstadt.

Population: 267,878 people

It will be divided into four districts: Braunschweig, Helmstadt, Hildesheim, Goslar.

6 The Department of the Saale

It will consist of the Principality of Blankenburg; of the County of Wernigerode; of the town of Quedlingburg with its area; of the Saalkreise; of those parts of Mansfeld which belonged to Prussia and to Saxony; and of some villages of the Duchy of Magdeburg.

Population: 206,222 people

Capital: Halberstadt

It will be divided into three districts: Halberstadt, Blankenburg, Halle.

7 The Department of the Werra

It will consist of the whole of Ober-Hessen; of the County of Ziegenhain; of the Principality of Hersfeld; of the greater part of Nieder-Hessen; and of the Herrschaft of Schmalkalden.

Population: 254,000

Capital: Marburg

It will be divided into three districts: Marburg, Hersfeld, Eschwege.

8 The Department of the Weser

It will consist of the Principality of Minden; the County of Ravensburg; of the Bistham Osnabrück; of the Hessian parts of Schaumburg; and of the Amt of Thedinghausen.

Population: 334,963 people

Capital: Osnabrück

It will be divided into four districts: Osnabrück, Minden, Bielefeld, Rinteln.

Signed: Hieronymus Napoleon

Hesse; and of the towns of Muhlhausen and Nordhausen.

Population: 210,989 people

Capital: Heiligenstadt

It will be divided into four districts: Heiligenstadt, Duderstadt, Osterode, Nordhausen.

4 The Department of the Leine

It will consist of the area of Göttingen, of part of the Principality of Grubenhagen and of parts of the *Länder* of Hildesheim, Braunschweig and Hesse.

Population: 145,537 people

Capital: Göttingen

It will be divided into two districts, Göttingen and Einbeck.

5 Department of the Ocker

It consists of almost all of the Principality of Wölfenbüttel; almost all of the Principality of

Berg and Westfalia were ruled completely according to French laws. Each district was divided into cantonments which were further divided into municipalities. A prefect ruled the Department and a sub-prefect each district. Cantons were headed by the canton-master and municipalities by community leaders. It must be admitted that this reorganization swept away many evils in the old system.

An edict of 31 March 1809 abolished the old distinctions between the nobility and the peasantry and petty bourgeoisie. On 12 November 1809 the Code Napoleon was introduced into the territories, bringing all citizens to equality before the law. The French laws also repealed unfair penalties against such religious minorities as the Jews. There were also disadvantages, however: free speech was suppressed, newspapers were censored, political articles were limited to those which appeared in the Paris Press and particularly the *Moniteur*. This was not all. War contributions and taxes were wrung from the people; billeting and supply of troops followed close on; and a state monopoly was declared on the sale of tobacco and salt.

Formation of the Army of Berg

Prior to 1806, the Duchy of Berg had belonged to Bavaria, and Bavarian rulers lie buried in Cologne's famous cathedral. When Napoleon amalgamated Berg with Kleve and parts of Münster and Nassau, certain army units also came to the new state from these vanished territories. They included the 12th Bavarian Line Infantry Regiment 'Kinkel', a battalion of the Nassau-Oranien infantry, and a detachment of Nassau-Oranien Hussars.

On 24 April 1806 the 1st Bergisch Infantry Regiment of four battalions was raised in Düsseldorf. Each battalion had eight companies each of 100 men. Many French soldiers were also drafted into this new regiment in order to ensure a degree of reliability. The French conscription system was introduced into Berg in October 1806, and on 29 August 1808 the single regiment was reorganized into two (the 1st and 2nd Regiments), each of three battalions containing six companies of 120 men. There was also a common depot battalion of four companies for recruit training.

In October 1808 the 3rd Regiment, also of three battalions, was raised. This infantry organization was maintained until 9 August 1811 when the 4th Regiment was raised from the three existing regiments. Now each regiment consisted of two battalions each containing eight companies (one grenadier, one voltigeur and six füsilier) of 120 men. Each regiment had in addition its own *Depot-Kompagnie*.

The cavalry of the duchy consisted initially of one regiment of light horse (*chevau-légers*) but on 1 April 1812 a second regiment was raised by transferring fifty troopers from the 1st Regiment and conscripting the rest.

There was also a battalion of artillery consisting of one company of horse artillery, one of foot artillery, one company of sappers, miners and pontoniers and one company of train.

Gendarmerie units on the French model were raised throughout the duchy and each city and town was required to provide its contingent of *garde national*.

Following the disastrous Russian campaign of 1812, Berg's troops were reduced to one weak infantry regiment of about 200 men, one cavalry regiment of one squadron, and two artillerymen. Berg fell under Prussian rule in 1813, and in May 1815 the infantry and cavalry were reconstituted. Of the two infantry regiments re-raised after 1812, the 1st Infantry Regiment of Berg became the 28th Prussian Line Infantry Regiment, and the 2nd Regiment became the 29th. The cavalry regiment became the 2nd Westfalian Hussars, Regiment No. 11. These numbers were retained until after the First World War.

Origins of the Westfalian Army

Of the old states which went to make up the infant kingdom of Westfalia in 1807 (Hanover, Braunschweig and Hessen-Kassel), only the latter had any troops to pass on to the new state. These were the men recruited by Marshal Mortier in October 1806 from the disbanded Hessian Army, to form the 'Franco-Hessian Infantry Corps'. In 1807 the two weak regiments of this formation were reorganized to form the 1st and 2nd Westfalian Line Infantry Regiments. When Jerome entered his new kingdom in December 1807 he was escorted by a detachment of Polish lancers. These men were transferred to Westfalian service and formed the basis of the 1st Squadron of the Chevau-légers of the Guard and of the Garde du Corps.

The 1st Light Battalion's cadre was formed of some hundreds of non-Prussians who had served in the Prussian Army and had been captured by the French in 1806. Napoleon had had them collected together at Küstrin and sent to Westfalia to help the rapid build-up of the Westfalian Army. This unit, consisting of a very mixed bag of men, was most unpopular in its garrison town of Kassel. Its misconduct reached such a level that it was transferred to Paderborn as a punishment – a town which even today serves as a garrison for German and British soldiers.

Westfalian general: a contemporary plate. (C. Suhr)

The remainder of the units of the Westfalian Army – with the exception of the Hussars of the Guard, who were of French origin – were raised and reinforced by drafts of conscripts. The French system of conscription was only one of a number of French features adopted: Westfalian soldiers wore French rank badges, answered to French titles, and were taught French drill and military discipline by French instructors.

Uniforms of the Westfalian Army

GENERALS
As for the French Army; dark blue coats with gold lace and buttons, gold sash, epaulettes and aiguilette; white breeches, high black boots, bicorns with gold edging, loop and button and white feather trim, sword with gold hilt on white slings.

THE GUARD
Garde du Corps. Gala uniform: white tunic, royal blue collar, lapels and cuffs all edged in red and bearing gold lace decoration; steel helmet with brass trim and combe, black crest and white plume on left-hand side, 'JN' on front plate; white breeches, high jacked boots, white gauntlets, gold buttons and gold fringeless epaulettes.

Service dress: same helmet (off duty a royal blue forage-cap with red piping and yellow grenade and lace could be worn); short-tailed, royal blue coat, red collar, turnbacks, cuffs and piping, gold lace to collar, cuffs and button-holes, gold shoulder-strap on the right shoulder; royal blue waistcoat and trousers, jacked boots. Trumpeters wore reversed colours and red plumes. Black bandolier and waist-belt with gold fittings and edging.
The Grenadier-Garde. See colour plates. Parade dress: black bearskins with red cords and plume and red top patch bearing a yellow grenade; white coat with long, red-lined skirts and red collar, lapels, cuffs and piping, yellow lace to collar, lapels and cuffs, yellow buttons; white trousers and white gaiters (black for winter and campaign wear), red epaulettes.

Field dress: shako with dark blue within white Westfalian cockade, red pompon, brass chin-scales and lozenge plate; single-breasted white coat with short red tails, red collar, cuffs and piping, red epaulettes. Off duty a plain bicorn and cockade were worn. Equipment was white crossbelts, black pouch with brass diamond plate and four grenades. French-pattern sabre with brass hilt and red knot. Officers wore a silver gorget with gold eagle badge and gold epaulettes, gold cords and white plumes to their bearskins. Drummers had red coats with white collars, cuffs, lapels and turnbacks, white swallow's nests edged in yellow and yellow lace edging to collar, cuffs and lapels; brass drum, white cords, dark blue hoops.

The Jäger-Garde. Shako with white eagle plate and cords, white plume, usual cockade (green forage-cap with yellow edging and horn badge); dark green coat with lemon-yellow collar, cuffs, turnbacks and edging to dark green lapels; white buttons, white lace on collar, cuffs, lapels and turnbacks. Green epaulettes, green breeches with white Hungarian thigh knots and white side-stripes, black short gaiters with white top trim and tassels. White belts, black pouch with white bugle badge, sabre with green knot.

The Chevau-légers-Garde. See colour plates. Black leather helmet with black crest and brass trim, red plume; short-tailed green jacket with red collar, cuffs, turnbacks and piping, yellow buttons, yellow lace to collar, cuffs and across the chest, yellow scale epaulettes and aiguilette. Green waistcoat and trousers, yellow Hungarian thigh knots and side trim, hussar boots with yellow trim and tassel. Trumpeters wore red coats, green collars and cuffs, red turnbacks with green piping, yellow lace on collars, cuffs and chest, hussar busbies with red cords, white plume and bag with yellow tassel; other items as for the troopers.

The Füsilier-Garde. See colour plates. As for the line infantry (white with dark blue facings) but white buttons and white lace decoration to collar, lapels and cuffs.

The Husaren-Garde ('The Lobsters'). See colour plates. Red shakos, white plumes, yellow shield plates, red dolman with yellow lace and buttons, blue (some sources say red) pelisses; red breeches with yellow trim.

Knötel plate of Westfalian National Guard, 1812

The Jäger-Carabinier-Bataillon. Shako with cockade, green plume with red tip, red cords, yellow eagle plate and chin-scales; dark green coat with red piping and turnbacks, dark green collar and cuffs, yellow buttons, dark green epaulettes with red half-moons, red lace decoration to collar and cuffs; dark green breeches with red Hungarian thigh knots and side-stripes, short black gaiters with red trim and tassel. Black crossbelts. red flask cord, brass-hilted *Hirsch-fänger* in brown sheath, rifles.

Artillery of the Guard. Shako with red cords, pompon and plume and yellow lozenge plate; royal blue jacket with seven red laces across the chest, red collar, cuffs, turnbacks and epaulettes; blue breeches with red Hungarian thigh knots and side-seams; hussar boots with red trim and tassel, buff gauntlets and bandolier.

THE LINE INFANTRY

Shakos with red pompons, cords and plumes for grenadiers (those of the 1st Regiment wore bear-skins as for the Grenadier-Garde); green cords and pompons and green plumes with yellow tips for voltigeurs; white cords and company colour pompons for the fusiliers (1st Company – light blue, 2nd – white, 3rd – yellow, 4th – green), yellow lozenge plate bearing the eagle over the black regimental number. White coats with facings shown on collar, cuffs, lapels and turnbacks, yellow buttons. Initially the regiments were differentiated by the facing colours (1st and 2nd – dark blue, 3rd and 4th – light blue, 5th and 6th – yellow), but in 1810 all facings became dark blue and regimental distinction was limited to the number raised on the buttons.

Grenadiers had red epaulettes, voltigeurs green and fusiliers initially had white shoulder-straps edged in the facing colour, but in 1812 this changed to dark blue epaulettes with white half-moons. Legwear was white breeches in knee-high black gaiters with black leather buttons. Equipment was white crossbelts, French sabre with knot according to company (grenadiers – red, voltigeurs – green, fusiliers – white) and rank (sergeants – mixed with gold, sergeant-majors – all gold). Drummers had red swallow's nests and their facings were edged in a coloured lace which varied according to regiment.

THE LIGHT INFANTRY
Their first uniforms were cornflower blue with green facings (soon changed to orange) and white buttons. This was soon changed to a dark green coat and trousers with light blue collar, pointed cuffs, turnbacks and piping, white buttons. Black belts, green breeches, black gaiters; shako with cockade, white eagle plate and green plume.

THE 1ST KÜRASSIERS (1806–12)
Steel helmet of French Kürassier pattern with black crest and brown fur turban; white tunic with crimson collar lapels, cuffs and turnbacks, white piping and buttons, red epaulettes, white breeches; high jacked boots. White belts, heavy cavalry swords, no kürasses until 1810 when French-pattern items were introduced.

1ST KÜRASSIER REGIMENT (1812–13)
As above but dark blue coat.

2ND KÜRASSIER REGIMENT
Helmet, breeches, boots, equipment and kürass as for the 1st Regiment; dark blue coat with orange facings and white buttons.

1ST CHEVAU-LÉGERS REGIMENT
Helmet as for the Chevau-légers-Garde, but with white fittings; dark green coat, orange collar, pointed cuffs, piping and turnbacks, white buttons; green breeches with orange Hungarian thigh knots (silver for officers) and side-stripes; black hussar boots with white trim and steel screw-in spurs. Officers wore silver and black bandoliers and silver edging to collar and cuffs and silver epaulettes. Trumpeters wore light blue coats with red facings and white lace; black for colbacks with green bag and white plume; and a light cavalry sabre. (A lance with white and blue pennant was introduced for a short time in 1811 and abandoned soon afterwards.)

Colonel Commandant of the Jäger-Carabiniers: a plate. (Alexander Sauerweid)

2ND CHEVAU-LÉGERS REGIMENT

As for the 1st Regiment but with buff facings.

1ST HUSSARS

Shako with cockade, white eagle plate and green plume, white chin-scales; green dolman pelisse and breeches with white buttons and lace and red collar and cuffs, black fur; red and white sash, black belts and sabretache with silver '1'. Trumpeters wore reversed colours. Brass-hilted light cavalry sabre in steel sheath.

2ND HUSSARS

As for the 1st Regiment but with light blue dolman, pelisse and breeches with red collar and cuffs and white shako plume and grey fur to pelisse; silver '2' on black sabretache.

THE ARTILLERY REGIMENT

Apart from the red collar this uniform was exactly as for the French artillery: shako with cockade, red pompon and cords and yellow plate; dark blue coat and trousers, dark blue lapels piped red, red collar, cuffs and turnbacks, yellow buttons; dark blue breeches with red Hungarian thigh knots; black gaiters, white belts.

THE TRAIN

Shako with cockade and white plate; grey coat with red collar, pointed cuffs and turnbacks, grey lapels piped red, white buttons; red waist-coats with white lace and buttons. Grey breeches, hussar boots. Officers had silver epaulettes and shako trim and silver bandoliers with red edging and silver plate bearing crossed cannons. Light cavalry sabre in steel sheath, hussar boots with silver trim.

THE GENDARMERIE

Once again, almost as for the French organization: bicorn with silver edging, cockade and red plume; dark blue coat with red collar, cuffs, lapels and turnbacks, white buttons and aiguilette; white breeches and high boots for mounted gendarmes, dark blue breeches and black gaiters for foot gendarmes, white belts.

THE DEPARTMENTAL COMPANIES

Bicorn with cockade; grey coat and trousers of infantry cut, grey collar and cuffs piped red; black gaiters, white buttons and belts.

THE NATIONAL-GARDE

The 1st Battalions of every town. Bicorn with cockade; long-skirted, dark blue coat with dark blue collar, cuffs and lapels all edged in red, red turnbacks. Blue trousers, white gaiters. Grenadiers had red epaulettes; black leatherwork. Voltigeurs wore green epaulettes with red half-moons; buttons were white. The 2nd Battalions had the same uniform but with white facings, mounted companies had red waistcoats with yellow buttons and lace.

Flags and Standards of the Westfalian Army

The infantry flags were of two patterns which differed only in that the inscriptions on the first were in French and on the second in German. The first flags were issued in 1808 and are known as 'M1808' pattern. They were square, dark blue with an upright white diamond in the centre. In each corner was a golden laurel wreath. The central diamond was edged in gold laurel leaves and bore on the face side the inscription 'LE ROI / DE WESTPHALIE / AU —BAT.' On the reverse was 'VALEUR / ET / DISCIPLINE'. Two years later the 'M1810' flags were issued; the design was the same but the inscriptions were now in German and in Gothic script. On the face side was 'DER KÖNIG / VON WESTPHALIEN / AM —REGIMENT'; on the reverse was 'TAPFERKEIT / UND / GUTES / BETRAGEN / —BAT'.

Standards came in four versions, M1808, M1812, M1812 (Guards) and M1813. These were all square and 60 centimetres along each side. The M1808 standard was dark blue with a white diagonal cross, on the face side was the royal monogram 'HN' and the Westfalian eagle, and on the reverse the Westfalian crest and mono-grams. The inscriptions were in French. The M1812 standard was the same as the M1808 but with German inscriptions. The M1812 (Guards) was only issued to the Garde du Corps, was in the same colours as the M1808 model, and was embroidered and edged with gold fringes. On the face side were four eagles and the central inscription 'DER KÖNIG / VON WESTPHALIEN / AN SEINE / LEIBGARDE ZU PFERDE'. On the reverse was the Westfalian crest with the monogram 'HN' in the corners. The M1813 standards were of a different design, vertically halved, dark blue (next to the pike) and white with German inscriptions.

Uniforms
of the Army of Berg

Initially, the infantry continued to wear their Bavarian uniforms, merely changing the light blue-within-white Bavarian cockade for the red-within-white one of Berg. This uniform consisted of the very tall, black leather casque with black woollen crest, round brass front plate bearing 'JMK' (Max Josef König (von Bayern)); cornflower-blue coat with black lapels and cuffs, red collar and turnbacks and piping to lapels and cuffs; white buttons, white trousers and belts, black gaiters, shoes and pouches. The brass-hilted sabre had a black sheath with brass tip.

Later in 1806 the uniform changed to a more French-style pattern. The shako replaced the casque and the Bavarian coat was discarded for the French spencer, closed to the waist with lapels buttoned back, in white. Light blue was the facing colour for all the four regiments and the distinguishing feature was the style of cuff. Buttons were yellow, belts white, packs brown calfskin, pouches black. The cockade remained red within white but shako plates seem to have varied. Three types appear to have been used: two were oval, one bearing the lion of Berg, the other the initial 'J', and the third was the standard lozenge eagle plate of the French Army.

Internal regimental organization seems to have been on the French pattern. Fusiliers wore trident-ended shoulder-straps in white, edged with light blue; grenadiers had bearskins with red cords and plumes and a white cross on a red background on top. They wore red epaulettes and had red sabre knots, whereas the fusilier sabre knot was light blue. Chasseurs had green pompons, white shako cords, green epaulettes with a red moon, and a green sabre strap with a red tassel. Rank badges were also on the French model and worn on the lower arm and round the top of the shako. Officers wore white French spencers faced in light blue with gold epaulettes according to rank, silver gorgets bearing the golden arms of the grand duchy, gold *porte-épée* and gold trim on the shako according to rank for junior officers; majors and above wore bicorns with gold trim and tassels. To protect the expensive white uniforms officers wore grey-beige surtouts and breeches while on campaign.

Drummers wore the distinguishing marks of their respective companies together with black coats with light blue collars, cuffs and turnbacks and a white lace with a red worm decoration to collar, cuffs and sleeves. Drums were yellow metal. Pioneers wore grenadier bearskins with red plumes and cords, red-fringed epaulettes and long white leather aprons edged in black fringes and decorated by a blue-within-white-within-red

Colonel Commandant of the Chevau-légers Lanciers of the Guard: a plate. (Alexander Sauerweid)

edging. They wore full beards and carried heavy axes, brass-hilted sabres with red knots, and carbines slung over their right shoulders. Grenadiers and voltigeurs wore moustaches, fusiliers were clean-shaven.

ARTILLERY

French infantry shako with red pompon and cords, brass shield-shaped plate bearing an 'N'. While Knötel shows the jacket to be almost of French artillery style (dark blue with red collar, shoulder-straps, cuffs and turnbacks, dark blue lapels and square cuff-flaps edged in red and with yellow buttons), a collection of pictures in the Von der Heydt Museum in Wuppertal painted by a Peter Schulten (who lived in that town and saw the troops passing through) shows a very Prussian-style coat (dark blue with black collar, cuffs, lapels, shoulder-straps and turnbacks all edged in red and with yellow buttons).

For parades, the horse artillery wore red plumes, dark blue breeches with a red side-stripe and short hussar boots with straight-necked, screw-in steel spurs. On campaign they wore grey buttoned overalls with red side-stripes. They had white pouch bandoliers and carried brass-hilted sabres in steel sheaths on white belts worn under the coat. The foot artillery wore red plumes, white cross-belts, and brass-hilted sabres with red knots; dark blue breeches within knee-high black gaiters with twelve brass buttons for parades, on campaign dark blue trousers with a red side-stripe over the gaiters.

THE TRAIN

French infantry shako with light blue pompon, red-within-white cockade, oval brass plate bearing a lion, brass chin-scales, no cords; grey coat with light blue collar, pointed cuffs, lapels and turnbacks, grey shoulder-straps piped light blue; black sabre bandolier, brass-hilted sabre in steel sheath, red knot. For parades grey breeches in short hussar-type boots with straight-necked, screw-in steel spurs; for campaign grey, buttoned overalls with light blue side-stripe worn over the boots.

THE CHEVAU-LÉGERS

This regiment's uniform and designation underwent several changes during its short life.

Initially it was termed the 'Chevau-légers du Grand Duc de Berg' (1807–8); then 'Chasseurs à Cheval du Grand Duché de Berg' (1808–9); 'Lanciers du Grand Duché de Berg' (1809–12); '1st and 2nd Regiments Chevau-légers du Grand Duché de Berg' (1812–13).

In the first role, although not armed with lances, they wore traditional lancer costume in white with pink facings edged in white, white buttons; pink-topped czapka with white cords and plume, red-within-white cockade, white front plate with yellow rays; pink breeches with double

Jerome Napoleon, King of Westfalia

white side-stripes, white belts and gauntlets, brass-hilted sabre in steel sheath, white sabre knot. Trumpeters wore reversed colours and had brass trumpets on silver cords and there was also a kettle-drummer, a Moor, in Arabian costume. Officers wore silver waist-sashes and silver cartouche belts and had silver sabre knots. On campaign in Spain they wore grey single-breasted coats with pink collar, cuffs and turnbacks and grey buttoned overalls with a pink side-stripe. The czapka was covered in black oilcloth.

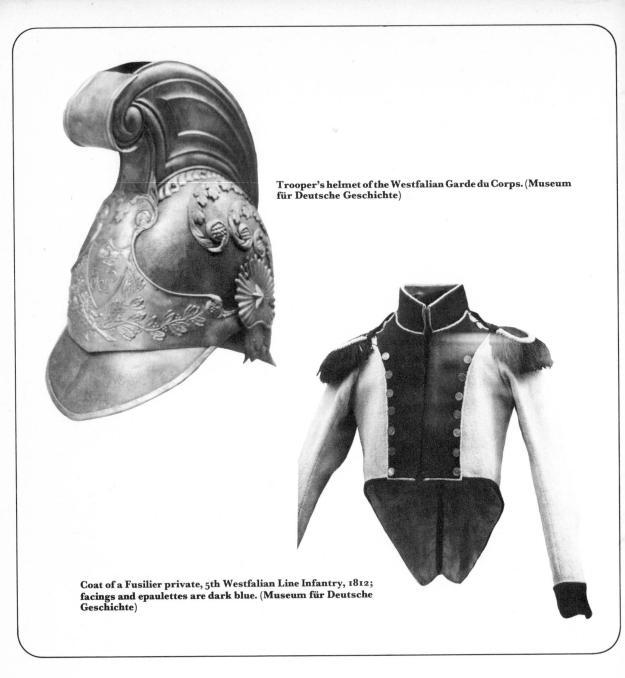

Trooper's helmet of the Westfalian Garde du Corps. (Museum für Deutsche Geschichte)

Coat of a Fusilier private, 5th Westfalian Line Infantry, 1812; facings and epaulettes are dark blue. (Museum für Deutsche Geschichte)

In the Chasseurs à Cheval role (1808–9) the uniform became dark green and the cut was no longer lancer-style. The collar, cuffs and turn-backs were pink, as was the piping to the dark green lapels and shoulder-straps. The élite company wore black sealskin colbacks with red plume, pompon, bag and tassel, and red epaulettes. Other companies wore black shakos with red-within-white cockade, company coloured pompon (1st Company – light blue, 2nd – white, 3rd – yellow, 4th – green) and diamond-shaped brass plate

bearing an eagle. Breeches were dark green and worn within hussar boots with red top trim and tassel. Gauntlets were white.

On 17 December 1809 the regiment was equipped with lances and retitled 'Lanciers du Grand Duché de Berg'. They wore the same dark green uniforms but adopted pink shakos with the same cockade and plate as before, and a white plume. For their action in overthrowing the Heavy Cavalry Brigade of the King's German Legion at Villadrigo on 23 October 1812 they were awarded the privilege of wearing pink-over-white pennons on their lances.

By 1812, as the 'Chevau-légers Lanciers', they were back in complete lancer costume in dark green with pink facings and white buttons and pink-topped czapkas. The élite company wore black fur colbacks and red epaulettes as before.

Flags and Standards of the Grand Duchy of Berg

There is very little evidence of the appearance of flags and standards or details of their issue. Murat designed the first flags and standards according to the following scheme: a red ground, round white central field edged in gold oak leaves and bearing the arms of the grand duchy, in each corner of the flag or standard a gold laurel wreath containing the regimental number; in the centre of each side a golden thunderbolt. The pike tip was a gilt spear-point. The motto on the scroll over the ducal crest was: 'Dieu, la Gloire, et les Dames'. It seems fairly certain that one standard of this design was presented to the regiment of Chevau-légers and one flag to the 1st Infantry Regiment 'Prince Joachim' in Düsseldorf in 1807. The standard seems to have gone to Naples with some of the men of the cavalry who accompanied Murat to his new throne in 1808. The 1st Chevau-légers did not receive another standard. The flag of the 1st Infantry Regiment was taken with the regiment to Spain in 1808, deposited in Figueres for safe keeping when the regimental strength became too low, and fell into Spanish hands when that town was captured. When the grand duchy passed into Napoleon's personal (effective) control, according to verbal tradition new flags were issued to the infantry in Düsseldorf, but the exact date is unknown. These flags were white and bore in the centre the Napoleonic eagle holding a thunderbolt in its claws. In two opposite corners were crowned 'N's, in a third corner the number

of the regiment, and in the fourth the number of the battalion. Below the eagle was the inscription: 'BRIGADE D'INFANTERIE DU GRAND DUCHÉ DE BERG' and above the eagle was: 'ET NOUS AUSSI, CÉSAR, CONDUIS-NOUS À LA VICTOIRE'. None of these flags has survived and it is most likely that they were destroyed or lost at the battle at the Beresina crossing in 1812.

The 2nd Regiment of Chevau-légers Lanciers apparently received a green standard, 60 centimetres high by 48 centimetres wide, bearing on the face side a silver grenade with gold flames between the gold initials 'B' and 'G', and on the reverse a number (2?) within gold laurel wreaths. This rather sketchy description is given by the Russian General Gekkel in his book describing the many trophies captured by the Russians in 1812 and laid up in the cathedral of Notre Dame de Kazan in Petrograd. The standard was lost at the Beresina crossing.

No flags or standards were issued to the new units raised by Berg in 1813.

Campaigns of the Westfalian Army

SPAIN 1808–13

Napoleon demanded Westfalian troops to support his campaign in Spain, initially requiring a division. By summer 1808 only one infantry regiment and the 1st Chevau-légers were ready. The cavalry regiment marched off in September 1808 with a strength of 500 men, but the desertion rate was high and only 390 men were still present when it reached the Spanish frontier. By spring 1809, however, the 2nd Division of the Westfalian Army was ready, and was sent southwards. They reached Perpignan on the Spanish border on 2 May 1809. Divisional organization was as follows:

Commander – Divisionsgeneral Graf Morio
Chief of Staff – Major von Hessberg
1st Brigade (Commander Brigadegeneral Boerner)
2nd Infantry Regiment (Oberst Legras – later Oberst von Bosse): two battalions.

4th Infantry Regiment (Oberst von Bonneville – later von Lassberg) : two battalions.

2nd Brigade (Commander Oberst von Ochs)

3rd Infantry Regiment (Oberst Zincke) : two battalions.

1st Light Battalion (Bataillonschef von Meyern).

Artillery (Bataillonschef Heinemann)

Two companies.

In Perpignan a depot under command of Major von Lassberg was set up. The Spanish War soon developed into a guerrilla campaign which sucked the life-blood out of Napoleon's occupying troops, and can be compared in effect to America's involvement in South Vietnam.

The Westfalians entered Spain on 5 May 1809 and were sent to join the besieging forces at Gerona under General Gouvion St Cyr. Arriving at Gerona next day, the 2nd Brigade was immediately involved in combat with the Spanish defenders of the town. As a result of their successful conduct in their baptism of fire, many men and officers were decorated and promoted, among them von Ochs (the brigade commander) who was promoted Brigadegeneral on 15 June 1809.

On 8 July 1809 Gerona was stormed with 3,000 men of the fourteen élite companies of the West-falian infantry regiments, the grenadier company of the 1st Neapolitan Infantry Regiment, twelve companies of the infantry of Berg (3rd Regiment)

Marshal Augereau

and Würzburg, and ten French élite companies). But the Spaniards beat off the attack and caused 1,770 casualties dead and wounded. Due to sickness among the Westfalian officers, von Ochs took command of the 2nd Division on 24 November 1809. On 31 August 1809 the Spanish General Blake attacked General St Cyr about seven miles south of Gerona. St Cyr ordered General Verdier (commander of the besiegers of Gerona) to join him with the bulk of his men. Verdier left only the Westfalian division, an Italian division and the regiments of Berg and Würzburg to cover the fortress and marched off south with the rest of the force. Blake promptly slipped round St Cyr, attacked the weakened besiegers, burned their camp, killed their wounded, and entered Gerona with a supply train of 1,500 mules. At Verdier's return, Blake pulled off into the mountains again.

Sickness and lack of food decimated the foreign troops attempting to subjugate Spain even more than the action of the enemy, and it was quite usual for entire companies to die in that country leaving none to report the state of affairs back to their homelands.

Gerona was stormed again (and in vain) on 19 September 1809 and cost the Westfalians and the Berg Infantry Regiment 9 officers and 124 men killed and wounded. These losses included the commander of the 3rd Berg Infantry Regiment, Oberst Muff. Gerona finally surrendered on 10 December 1809 having been starved into submission.

The Westfalian division then numbered 1,500 of all ranks; but on 12 March 1810 they were joined by 650 reinforcements from Westfalia. General St Cyr was replaced in command of the French Army of Catalonia by Augereau in October 1809; by the spring of 1810 Augereau had subdued the province and marched to Barcelona. The Westfalians, who remained to garrison Gerona, were subjected to ceaseless guerrilla attacks which reduced their strength so much that in May 1809 the 1st Battalions were made up to strength by men of the 2nd Battalions, and remained in Spain, while the cadres of the 2nd Battalions of the regiments were sent back to Westfalia to recruit up to strength again.

Augereau was replaced by Marshal Macdonald in May 1810, but the position in Spain continued

A contemporary English cartoon pokes fun at Napoleon's 'newly baked' Confederation of the Rhine

o deteriorate. On 1 April 1811 the 1st Battalions of the Westfalian units were withdrawn home to recruit, and there remained in Spain only one battalion of 500 men (composed of those men of all units who were still fit for duty) and an artillery detachment. These units did not return home until spring 1813.

The Westfalian Chevau-léger Regiment had never operated with the Westfalian division in Spain; initially it was attached to Victor's I Corps and later was transferred to Sebastiani's IV Corps. It was involved in many skirmishes and battles and won great fame. The first commander of the regiment, Oberst von Hammerstein, returned to Westfalia on 16 July 1810 to be replaced by Oberst von Stein.

In February 1813 the main part of the regiment returned to Westfalia, but one squadron remained in Spain under command of Eskadronschef von Plessen. This unit was (like all other German satellite units) declared unreliable by the French, disarmed, and interned as prisoners of war on 3 December 1813.

THE 1809 CAMPAIGN IN NORTHERN GERMANY

Austria declared war on France on 9 April 1809 and placed the weight of her forces in southern Germany and Italy. Only secondary forces were deployed in the north, against Westfalia and, to combat this threat, King Jerome was given command of X Corps of the First German Army on 18 April. In addition to the Austrian threat to the east, Jerome had also to keep an eye on the northern coast to guard against possible British landings.

The composition of X Corps was as follows:

Commander, King Jerome
Chief of Staff, the Westfalian General Rewbell
1st Westfalian Division of the Guard (Divisionsgeneral Graf Bernterode)
One squadron Garde du Corps of 140 men commanded by Brigadegeneral von Bongars
One battalion Grenadier-Garde of 840 men commanded by Oberst Langenschwarz
One battalion Jäger-Garde of 600 men commanded by Major Füllgraf

Eugéne Beauharnais, Viceroy of Italy – the man who finally led the remnant of the Grand Armée back to Germany

Also coming to join Jerome from the West were, under command of Oberst Chabert:

3rd Regiment of Berg Infantry (1,000 men)

Detachments of the 22nd, 27th, 30th, 33rd and 65th French Line Infantry and 28th Light Infantry regiments and of the 6th, 7th and 8th Artillery Regiments – 3,000 men in all

The Prussian fortresses of Stettin, Stralsund and Küstrin were garrisoned with Rheinbund troops – 2,300 Mecklenburgers and 800 Oldenburgers. But these troops could not be removed from the fortresses to support Jerome in his field operations.

A detailed account of this campaign in North Germany appears in *The Black Brunswickers* (see Sources) so only details concerning the armies of Westfalia and Berg will be given here.

On 4 May 1809 the Westfalian General von Uslar, with a force of 1,000 men (four companies of the 1st Westfalian Infantry Regiment, two companies of the 22nd French Infantry Regiment under Oberst Legat, and two guns) moved to Dodendorf to block von Schill's advance. Due to the bad state of readiness of the 5th and 6th Westfalian Infantry Regiments at this time (they were still in training) General von Uslar was removed from command that day and replaced by Oberst Vauthier. Von Schill's Freikorps with 400 hussars, 60 *Reitende Jäger* (mounted rifles) and 50 infantry advanced on Dodendorf from Sulldorf. Vauthier left his defensive position behind the River Sulze, advanced to meet von Schill, and formed his men into three squares (two in front, one in reserve) with his two guns in front of the front two squares.

Von Schill's cavalry charged, broke the squares at the first impact, and captured 200 men and both guns. Oberst Vauthier was badly wounded, captured, released by Schill, and died later in Magdeburg. The Westfalian Gendarmerie had great trouble rounding up their scattered soldiers after the battle, many of whom took the opportunity to return to their homes. Legat's grenadier company, which was in reserve behind Dodendorf, was also captured by von Schill's men. The Dutch Division after the Austrians next day. But Jerome men, while the Westfalians remained at Dömitz on the Elbe to regroup.

On 18 June 1809 Jerome left Kassel with the

Three squadrons Chevau-légers-Garde of 550 men commanded by Oberst Wolff

One battalion Jäger-Carabiniers of 360 men commanded by Prinz von Hessen-Philippsthal

Total 2,490 men

2nd Westfalian Division (Divisionsgeneral d'Albignac)

1st Infantry Regiment of 1,680 men commanded by Oberst Vauthier (killed at Dodendorf)

5th Infantry Regiment of 1,800 men commanded by Oberst Graf Wellingerode

6th Infantry Regiment of 1,700 men commanded by Major von Bosse

1st Kürassier Regiment of 260 men commanded by Oberst von Würthen

Total 5,440 men

3rd Dutch Division (Divisionsgeneral Gratien)

6th Dutch Infantry Regiment

7th Dutch Infantry Regiment

8th Dutch Infantry Regiment

9th Dutch Infantry Regiment

2nd Dutch Kürassier Regiment

Three companies of artillery

Total 5,300 men

Thus the grand total of X Corps was 10,263 men.

Guards Division to march eastwards. His mission was to help King Friedrich August of Saxony whose city of Dresden had been occupied by General Am Ende's Austrian forces on 11 June 1809. By 21 June Jerome was at Eisenach, and had the divisions of d'Albignac and Gratien join him; thus his total force was 12,900 men, increased the following day by 2,000 Saxons.

On 24 June Jerome advanced from Sondershausen towards Querfurt, crossed the River Saale, and entered Merseburg. Meanwhile the Austrians had occupied Leipzig; Jerome sent the 2nd Westfalian Division against them and the Austrians withdrew again. He then entered Leipzig on 26 June with three divisions, and sent the Dutch Division after the Austrians next day. But Jerome was outwitted by the rapid movements of the Austrians and their Black Brunswick allies, and was always at least one move behind in his dispositions. From 1 to 4 July he stayed in Dresden, celebrating his strategic successes while the enemy rampaged in the Nürnberg area. Finally he moved out of the city comforts he loved so much (his nickname was 'König Lustig' (the Merry Monarch) and marched south to Chemnitz. His aim was to join up in Hof with Junot's corps,

coming north-east out of Franconia with over 10,000 men and pushing the Austrian General Kienmayer before him.

Kienmayer broke contact, turned on Jerome, and overthrew him at Berneck and Gefraess on 8 July. On 11 July X Corps was checked again by the Austrians near Hof. Jerome fell back on Schleitz, where Kienmayer again pushed him aside on 13 July. By 17 July X Corps had withdrawn to Erfurt when news of the armistice between Austria and France (due to the Austrian defeat at Wagram 5 and 6 July 1809) reached Jerome. Full of relief, Jerome hurried back to his capital, Kassel, with his guard. The Dutch Division remained in Erfurt. The remaining Westfalian troops under General Rewbell went to Hanover in pursuit of the Black Brunswickers, who were fighting their way up towards Bremen to be shipped to England on British ships.

General Rewbell, with the 1st Kürassiers, 1st and 6th infantry regiments, the 3rd Bergisch infantry regiment, and ten guns, was to have been joined by the 5th Westfalian Infantry Regiment from Magdeburg, but this unit was destroyed at Halberstadt on 29 July by the Black Brunswickers; 1,500 men of the 5th were killed, wounded or captured (300 of these crossed over to the Black Brunswickers) and only about 100 escaped. Their flags were also captured, but what became of them is not known. Rewbell moved to Celle on 31 July 1809 to cut the Brunswickers off from the coast, and on 1 August a skirmish took place with them at Oelper (nowadays absorbed in the town complex of Brunswick). After initial success, Rewbell's men were repulsed. The Kürassiers suffered heavily from artillery fire, fell back under pursuit by the Brunswick hussars, rode over their own infantry, and nearly caused a disaster. Only the brave conduct of the Westfalian gunners prevented the enemy exploiting this advantage.

The chase up to Bremen was then resumed, with Rewbell making haste slowly in order to keep a safe distance between himself and his quarry. In this he succeeded so well that the Brunswickers were even able to sell their horses before embarking for England, at Brake on the Weser, on 8 August 1809. Suspecting that he might suffer Jerome's rage for his failure in this campaign, Rewbell took ship for America.

Josephine Beauharnais, Napoleon's first wife

Russia, 1812

Much has been written about this ill-fated venture, one of the most dramatic and tragic military events of modern times. The Grande Armée of 1812 contained, as well as French troops, Rheinbund Germans, Poles, Prussians, Austrians, Spaniards, Portuguese, Italians, Neapolitans, Swiss and Croats. Over half the men involved were non-French.

The Westfalian Army formed its own corps (VIII). The troops of Berg became part of IX Corps.

The composition of VIII Corps was as follows:

Commander, King Jerome
Executive Commander, Divisionsgeneral Vandamme (a French officer appointed by Napoleon).

23RD DIVISION (Commander, Divisionsgeneral von Ochs)
1st Brigade (Commander, initially Brigadegeneral Graf Wellingerode; from May 1812 Brigadegeneral Legras)
Grenadier-Garde, 1 battalion (Oberst Legras)
Jäger-Garde, 1 battalion (Major Picot)
Jäger-Carabiniers, 1 battalion (Major Müldner)
1st Light Infantry Battalion (Bataillonschef von Rauschenplatt)
5th Line Infantry Regiment, 2 battalions (Oberst Gissot)
2nd Brigade (Commander, Brigadegeneral Danloup-Verdun)
1st Line Infantry Regiment, 2 battalions (Oberst Plessmann)
8th Line Infantry Regiment, 2 battalions (Oberst Bergeron)
4th Line Infantry Regiment, 2 battalions (Oberst Rossi)
24TH DIVISION (Commander, Divisionsgeneral Thareau
1st Brigade (Commander, Brigadegeneral Damas)
6th Line Infantry Regiment, 2 battalions (Oberst Ruelle)
2nd Line Infantry Regiment, 3 battalions (Oberst von Füllgraff)
3rd Light Infantry Battalion (Oberst von Hessberg)
2nd Brigade (Commander, Brigadegeneral von Zurwesten (from 2 July 1812 von Borstell))
3rd Line Infantry Regiment, 2 battalions (Oberst Bernard)

David's portrait of the Emperor in 1810. He is wearing his favourite uniform of a Colonel of the Guard

7th Line Infantry Regiment, 3 battalions (Oberst Lageon)

2nd Light Infantry Battalion (Bataillonschef von Bodicker)

Garde-Kavallerie-Brigade (Commander, Brigadegeneral Wolff)

Garde du Corps, 1 squadron (Eskadronschef Lallemand)

Chevau-léger-Garde, 4 squadrons (Oberst Müller)

(When the Garde du Corps returned to Kassel with King Jerome in August 1812, the Chevau-léger-Garde was attached to the Leichte-Kavallerie-Brigade.)

Leichte-Kavallerie-Brigade (Commander, Brigadegeneral von Hammerstein)

1st Hussars, 4 squadrons (Oberst von Zandt)

2nd Hussars, 4 squadrons (Oberst von Hessberg)

Schwere-Kavallerie-Brigade (Commander, Brigadegeneral von Lepel)

1st Kürassiers, 4 squadrons (Oberst von Gila)

2nd Kürassiers, 4 squadrons (Oberst von Bastineller)

Artillerie (Commander, Divisionsgeneral Allix)

1st Reitende Batterie der Garde

1st Reitende Batterie

Two foot batteries

Four Train companies

Twelve regimental pieces (six-pounders)

Six reserve guns

A total of forty-eight cannons

The entire contingent numbered as follows:

	Men	*Horses*	*Guns*
Infantry	22,315	*	12
Cavalry	3,374	3,659	
Artillery	997	*	36
Train	588	1,196	
Baggage	324	1,206	
General staff, gendarmerie, etc.	254	*	
Totals	27,852	6,061*	48

* The horses of mounted officers; adjutants, etc., are not shown.

This organization soon changed, however.

In Warsaw in June 1812 the Schwere-Kavallerie-Brigade was detached and became part of IV Cavalry Corps. The 1st and 8th Line Infantry Regiments were detached and transferred to X Corps and went into Danzig as garrison troops. The 4th Line Infantry Regiment was detached to become part of XI Corps of the 'Duna Army'. These detachments reduced VIII Corps to 22,392 men, 4,284 horses and 44 guns.

On 4 March 1812 VIII Corps marched off from Kassel; by 6 April they were at Glogau, and on 13 April at Rawitsch. There Jerome assumed command of the right wing of the Grande Armée, consisting of V Corps (Poniatowski and the Poles), VII Corps (the Saxons under General Reynier), VIII Corps and IV Cavalry Corps (Latour-Mauborg). In all this force totalled 80,000 men.

Napoleon's strategy for 1812 was to make a rapid advance into Russia, catch the two Russian armies separated, and destroy them in detail before they could unite. This meant forced marches for the troops through very poor areas with few (and bad) roads. The logistics vehicles of the Grande Armée failed to keep up with the forward troops, hundreds died of exhaustion, thirst, starvation and suicide and the organization of the forward elements became completely weak and confused. As one Württemberg officer wrote in his diary: 'What will happen if we catch up with the enemy?'

There was little danger of this, however. The two Russian armies withdrew eastwards in excellent order, leaving no stragglers or booty behind them, and they devastated the areas which they had to sacrifice to the invaders.

Relationships between Jerome and Vandamme were very bad. Vandamme had the men's welfare at heart and constantly interfered with Jerome's plans in order to ensure that all units had sufficient food. Finally, in Grodno, Jerome's patience came to an end, and he dismissed Vandamme. Both then appealed to the Emperor who, more out of family loyalty than good judgement, sent Vandamme back to France. General Thareau took over command of VIII Corps on 6 June for about four weeks until Marshal Junot arrived to replace him.

On 13 July VIII Corps reached Nieswitz in a most exhausted condition and Jerome allowed his troops a few days' well-earned rest. To date only cavalry skirmishes had taken place with the Russians and these had all ended in defeats for the invaders.

The two Russian armies were now able to unite and Napoleon's hope of an early victory was dashed. Even though that wing of the Grande Armée under Marshal Davout had also failed to catch their allotted Russians, Napoleon poured out his rage on Jerome. This unhappy monarch was sent packing back to Kassel with his Garde du Corps on 16 July, and Junot was left in command of VIII Corps with Davout replacing Jerome. That same day the advance continued towards Minsk and reached Orscha on 27 July, where a fourteen-day halt was called. By this time VIII Corps had lost over 2,000 men due to sickness and exhaustion, and on 11 August a reinforcement draft of 1,200 infantry and 300 cavalry joined them from Westfalia. The advance on Smolensk began again on 12 August and on the 15th it appeared that the Russians under Barclay de Tolly and Bagration were prepared to give Napoleon the battle which he so urgently required.

The task of enveloping the Russian left wing was given to VIII Corps, but Junot got lost, granted his men six hours' rest, and thus missed the battle, reaching the battlefield only at 10 p.m. on 17 August.

Joachim, Prince Murat, Napoleon's dashing but unreliable brother-in-law, Grand Duke of Berg and later King of Naples

The Emperor quivered with rage at this lax conduct but gave Junot, his old comrade, a further chance: VIII Corps was to cut off the Russian rearguard (they had evacuated and burned Smolensk) and destroy it on 19 August. Junot crossed the Dniepr River but then decided to allow his corps to rest in the village of Szenkowo.

Meanwhile, Ney was locked in fierce combat with the enemy rearguard at Valutina-Gora. Eventually the Westfalians appeared on the Russian left flank (which was not prepared for an assault from this direction) but instead of attacking and utilizing his surprise, Junot set about deploying his troops into columns. The Russians realized their peril, changed front and thus avoided destruction. Murat, King of Naples, saw Junot's delay and galloped across the battlefield in a fury to order him to assault at once. This he did, but the attack was ill-timed and the voltigeurs of the 2nd Westfalian Light Battalion were cut down by a Cossack charge.

Total Westfalian casualties at Valutina-Gora were 450 all ranks killed, wounded and captured.

Junot's second failure exhausted the Emperor's patience with him and as a punishment VIII Corps was detailed to form the rearguard of the army and to clear the battlefield of Smolensk, which took them from 20 to 22 August. French and Allied dead and wounded were reckoned to have been 20,000 in this battle and the Russian casualties 'surely more'.

On 24 August VIII Corps moved off towards Moscow and suffered much hunger due to the fact that the preceding troops had stripped and plundered everything of use from the area over which they now had to travel. They marched via Dorogobusch, Vyazma and Gschatz to Mozhaisk which they reached on 6 September 1812.

After having detached three battalions and two squadrons to form outposts along the lines of communication, the strength of VIII Corps was now fifteen battalions, ten squadrons and six batteries of artillery – 10,000 men in all.

THE BATTLE OF BORODINO,
7 SEPTEMBER 1812

The Russian Army had taken up a prepared position just west of Moscow with the aim of denying the invaders access to their capital city.

Alexander I, Tsar of Russia

The Battle of Hohenlinden, 3 December 1800; this French victory caused the collapse of the rotten Holy Roman Empire of German nations

This gave Napoleon the battle he had so long desired, and he set about achieving the destruction of the opposing army.

The position of VIII Corps was on the right of the Grande Armée behind III Corps of Marshal Ney. At about 7.30 a.m. VIII Corps advanced to storm the Semenowskoje Redoubt, and were attacked by kürassiers as they left the cover of some woods. The Westfalians formed square and repulsed the kürassiers, causing them considerable losses. Meanwhile, V Corps was forced back by the Russians, and VIII Corps now suffered heavily from artillery fire. General Damas was killed, General Thareau was badly wounded, and General von Ochs took over command of the 23rd Division. Now, III Corps attacked the Semenowskoje Redoubt, was repulsed, and by 9 a.m. the battle was deadlocked.

The assault was renewed by III, VIII and V (Polish) Corps, and by 11 a.m. the Semenowskoje Redoubt had been captured. Shortly afterwards the Rajewski Redoubt on the left flank was also captured.

A slow advance followed, and at one point General von Ochs led a charge with himself at the head of the 6th Westfalian Line Infantry Regiment. The Russians, fighting stubbornly, withdrew in good order eastwards into the woods. By 5 p.m. the firing slackened and the battle ended in Napoleon's favour.

It had been a bloody day. The losses of VIII Corps were 18 officers and 488 men dead, and 164 officers and 2,340 men wounded, of which at least one-third subsequently died of their wounds. Heaviest losses had been suffered by the three light cavalry regiments in their charges on the redoubt. Generals Thareau and von Lepel died of their wounds. French losses were 30,000 dead and wounded, including 49 generals; Russian losses are given by the French as being about 50,000 dead, wounded and captured.

At midday on 8 September, Napoleon moved off towards Moscow, firmly believing that once this prize was in his hands, Russia would fall at his feet. How great his disappointment was to be.

Once again the unlucky VIII Corps was given

24

Grand Duchy of Kleve-Berg:
1 Füsilier, 1st Infantry Regiment, 1807–8
2 Drummer of grenadiers, 2nd Infantry Regiment, 1807
3 Sergeant-major colour-bearer, 1st Infantry Regiment, 1808

MICHAEL ROFFE

A

Grand Duchy of Kleve-Berg:
1 Chevau-légers Lancier, campaign dress,
  1812–13
2 Chevau-légers Lancier, Compagnie d'Elite,
  full dress, 1812
3 Lieutenant, 2nd Infantry Regiment,
  campaign dress, 1808–13

B

MICHAEL ROFFE

Grand Duchy of Kleve-Berg:
Chevau-légers, full dress, 1807

Kingdom of Westfalia:
1 Trumpeter, Garde du Corps, 1812
2 Grenadier of the Grenadier-Garde, review order, 1812
3 Jäger of the Jäger-Garde, review order, 1812

D

Kingdom of Westfalia:
1 Driver, Military Train, 1812
2 Officer, 1st Hussars, 1812
3 Trumpeter, 2nd Hussars, 1812

MICHAEL ROFFE

E

1

2

3

Kingdom of Westfalia:

1 **Officer of grenadiers, line infantry,
  campaign dress,** 1812
2 **Officer of light infantry,** 1812
3 **Officer of grenadiers, Infantry Regiment
  'Königin',** 1812

F

Kingdom of Westfalia:
1 Trooper, Chevau-légers-
    Garde, 1812
2 Officer, 1st Kürassiers, 1808
3 Corporal of voltigeurs, line
    infantry, 1812

Kingdom of Westfalia:
1 Gunner, Horse Artillery of the Guard, 1812
2 Officer, Foot Artillery, 1812
3 Trooper, Hussars 'Jerome Napoleon', 1813

Eyewitness impression of the Battle of Borodino by Faber du Four

the task of clearing the grisly battlefield. The plight of the unfortunate wounded was so bad, and medical facilities so limited, that the Westfalians were ordered to carry out mercy killings on the obviously hopeless cases. On 12 September VIII Corps moved off and Junot set up his headquarters in the town of Mozhaisk. The only Westfalian troops to enter Moscow were the Kürassier Brigade, and an infantry brigade consisting of the 3rd Line Infantry Regiment and the 2nd and 3rd Light Battalions.

Due to the lack of food in Mozhaisk, Junot was forced to disperse VIII Corps all along the lines of communication from Dorogobusch to Moscow. This dispersal laid the isolated units open to attack by Cossack and peasant militia bands. On 10 October, 450 men of the 1st Battalion of the 6th Line Infantry Regiment under Bataillonschef von Conrady were surprised in the town of Vereja by a Russian force under General Dorochow, and captured together with their battalion flag.

Just before the notorious retreat from Moscow began, the 8th Line Infantry Regiment rejoined VIII Corps from Danzig with 1,000 men, and a reinforcement draft from Westfalia also arrived. This brought the corps' strength up to 5,600 infantry and 600 cavalry, with all guns still present.

On 28 October the retreat began, and the headquarters of VIII Corps left Mozhaisk. The corps was now the Advanced Guard of the Grande Armée.

They marched over the battlefield of Borodino in mild weather, picking their way carefully between the heaps of unburied dead and the rotting carcasses of horses.

By 4 November the troops had eaten up the last of the food they had managed to bring with them, and the weather became much colder with snowfalls. Because the Russians forced Napoleon to withdraw through the same devastated area over which he had advanced, almost no food could be scavenged by the troops as they marched, and casualties due to men collapsing from starvation and fatigue rose alarmingly day by day. To add to the misery of the retreating troops, bands of Cossacks and armed peasants were ever lurking to fall upon small bands of men searching for food away from the protection of the main body of the army.

The men were often plodding along in deep mud, until 2 December when the weather became very cold and frozen.

On 5 November the Westfalians passed through Dorogobusch and, on the 8th, Smolensk. Shortly before this town, at Valutina-Gora, on an icy hill, all their cannon and most of the baggage had to be abandoned because the horses were too weak (and unsuitably shod) to pull their loads up the glassy slope. On 9 November VIII Corps had shrunk to 1,700 men, and in Smolensk it was reorganized into three battalions. On 13 November they marched out of Smolensk and had to fight their way through a Russian force which blocked their path. That night, VIII Corps was down to 500 combatants under Divisionsgeneral von Ochs.

By 22 November the weather had become much milder and heavy rain made the march even more difficult than before. Now only 120 infantry men remained under arms, and 'VIII Corps' became one weak battalion and a cavalry squadron also of about 120 men.

The Westfalians reached Borissow on the Beresina River on 26 November, and the river was crossed on the 28th, General von Ochs with fifty infantry and General von Hammerstein with sixty mounted cavalrymen. Some days later, Hammerstein with his cavalry was able to rescue the wounded Marshal Oudinot from a Russian raiding force of Cossacks.

In Wilna VI Corps (Bavarians) rejoined the main body of the Grande Armée and with them was the relatively intact 4th Westfalian Line Infantry Regiment. This unit was thrust into the fight and rapidly destroyed at Rukoni on 9 December 1812.

On 12 December Kowno was reached, and next day the Prussian border. After the crossing of the River Niemen the Russian pursuit slackened.

Friedrich Wilhelm, 'Black Duke' of Brunswick, pictured in a bivouac during his 1809 campaign in Westfalia

The town of Thorn was designated as rendezvous for the surviving Westfalians, and during January 1813 184 officers and 683 men straggled in from Russia. They were reinforced by 1,294 men from the depots in Westfalia.

Soon the 1st and 2nd Marschregimenter (temporary tactical units) were organized and the new VIII Corps was commanded by General von Füllgraf. General von Hammerstein had returned to Westfalia to organize the rebuilding of the cavalry. On 16 January the Marschregimenter became the new 4th and 5th Line Infantry Regiments, and on 12 February were sent to Küstrin only to be besieged in that place which capitulated on 20 March 1814.

In fact the Westfalians did not eventually form a corps for the 1813 campaign. They took the field in small combat groups, each of which operated independently, and the number 'VIII' passed to the Poles.

The 1st Line Infantry Regiment had been detached from VIII Corps in 1812, had taken part in the Siege of Riga, and withdrew into Prussia on 27 December 1812 having suffered only slight losses. On 5 January 1813 it entered Danzig and was besieged there until that place surrendered on 29 November 1813. It was then taken into Prussian service as the Reserve Bataillon des Elbregiments, which subsequently combined with the Jäger-Bataillon 'von Reiche' and the infantry of von Hellwig's Stveifkorps on 31 March 1815 to form the 27th Prussian Infantry Regiment. This number was retained until 1918. The 1st Infantry Regiment was the only Westfalian unit to survive the extinguishing of the kingdom in 1813.

The 2nd and 3rd Infantry Regiments and the 2nd Light Battalion went into Dresden as garrison troops and were captured and disbanded when that town fell. The 4th and 5th Infantry Regiments were, as already related, captured at the fall of Küstrin. The 6th Infantry Regiment was not re-raised after 1812. The 7th Infantry Regiment was disbanded at the dissolution of the kingdom. The 8th Infantry Regiment, the 1st and 4th Light Battalions and the newly raised Füsilier-Garde (also called the 'Regiment Königin') were disbanded after the Battle of Leipzig (18 October 1813); and the newly raised 9th Line Infantry Regiment suffered a similar fate. The 1st and 2nd Hussar Regiments went over to the Austrians on the night of 22/23 August 1813 near Zittau, and became the 1st and 2nd Hussars of the Austro-German Legion. They were subsequently disbanded.

The Garde du Corps, Grenadier-Garde, Jäger-Garde, Jäger Carabiniers, Chevau-légers-Garde, Garde-Husaren-Regiment 'Jerome Napoleon' (a collection of French recruits presented to Jerome by the Emperor), the artillery, the 3rd Light Battalion, 1st and 2nd Kürassier Regiments and the 1st Chevau-légers Regiment were all in Westfalia when the end of Jerome's regime came in September 1813, and they melted away into the anonymity of the civilian populace.

So ended the kingdom of Westfalia. On 21 November 1813 the Kurfürst (Prince Elector) of Hessen-Kassel re-entered his old capital city, Kassel, from which he had been banned in 1806, and his realm was re-created for him by the great powers. The rest of Westfalia reverted to its original owners – the Duke of Brunswick (Braunschweig), the King of England (the Elector of Hanover) and the King of Prussia. Few mourned the passing of the state which Napoleon had created for his brother, but its army had won the respect of many of its friends and foes during its short life.

Campaigns of the Troops of Berg

1806–7

As early as 1806 a regiment of infantry left the grand-duchy and took the field against the Prussian fortresses which still held out after most of the Prussian field army had been destroyed. They operated with the Regiment 'Würzburg' at the Siege of Graudenz in June 1807.

1809 (GERMANY)

The 3rd Infantry Regiment formed part of Vaufreland's brigade in Legrange's 3rd Division

27

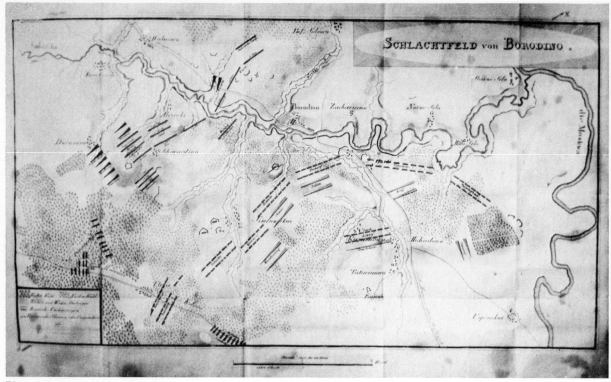

Plan of the battlefield of Borodino

of General Junot's Reserve Corps, and their employment has already been mentioned in the corresponding section of the battle history of the Westfalian Army. The other infantry units of this brigade were the 65ᵉ Ligne and the 46ᵉ Ligne.

SPAIN

In February 1808 two squadrons of the 1st Chevau-légers went to Spain, and on 17 November of that year they were attached to the Imperial Guard in Madrid. They remained with the Guard throughout their stay in Spain.

On 29 December 1808 they fought at Benavente and were active in northern Spain. In 1810 they distinguished themselves at Yanguas on 6 September and at Villafranca on 26 December. On 5 May 1811 they were part of Montbrun's force which charged the British at Fuentes de Onoro and later that year they fought at Burgos and Cuidad Rodrigo.

On 23 October 1812 they charged with the French 15ᵉ Chasseurs à Cheval and the Gendarmes of Burgos to overthrow General Anson's Heavy Cavalry Brigade of the King's German Legion at Villadrigo. As a reward for this victory, Napoleon permitted them to wear red and white silk lance pennants.

The 1st Infantry Regiment also went to Spain in 1809, as did the 2nd Infantry. They served at the Siege of Gerona, and suffered casualties of 605 out of 1,310 and 709 out of 1,313 respectively between 1 June and 15 September 1809. In 1810 the 3rd Infantry also went to Spain, but at the end of the following year the cadres of the 1st and 2nd Regiments and of the 1st Battalion of the 3rd Regiment returned to Germany. All serviceable soldiers were gathered in the 2nd Battalion of the 3rd Regiment, which remained in Spain until 1813.

1812

For the Russian invasion in 1812 Berg provided the following troops:

Infantry Commander, General Geither
1st Line Infantry Regiment, 2 battalions
2nd Line Infantry Regiment, 2 battalions
3rd Line Infantry Regiment, 1 battalion (the 2nd Battalion was still in Spain)
4th Line Infantry Regiment, 2 battalions

28

The Prussian Marshal Blücher and the Allied monarchs at Leipzig, 18 October 1813, after the fateful battle

Cavalry Commander, Oberst Graf von Nesselrode
2nd Chevau-légers Lanciers Regiment, 4 squadrons
Artillery Battalion
    One horse artillery battery
    One foot artillery battery
    One company of sappers, miners and pontoniers
    One train company
Total 5,000 men

The company of sappers and miners was attached to the Imperial Guard, and all members of the company died in Russia.

The main body of the Berg troops were attached to IX Corps of Marshal Victor, which was initially part of the Grande Armée's reserve in Prussia and Warsaw. General Damas was appointed commander-in-chief of the Berg Brigade which with some Baden regiments formed the 26th Infantry Division under Divisionsgeneral Dändels. The 2nd Berg Chevau-légers Lanciers were brigaded with the Garde-Chevau-légers of Hessen-Darmstadt and became the 30th Light Cavalry Brigade under General Delaitre.

In September 1812 IX Corps lay round Kowno, but Napoleon now ordered them to advance into Russia to take up the shattered survivors currently withdrawing from Moscow. Moving to Smolensk, IX Corps stayed there until mid-October, and then marched east again towards the Duna River. By the time they reached their junction-point with the Grande Armée at Losnitza, IX Corps had lost one-third of its men but was still in relatively good condition. The Berg Brigade had now lost all its artillery, and one complete battalion had been captured in Vitebsk. Now IX Corps became rearguard of the Grand Armée, marched to the Beresina at Borissow, and then moved north to Studienka. In order to secure the withdrawal of the main body of Napoleon's remaining troops westwards over this obstacle, IX Corps crossed the notorious bridges which Napoleon had had built at this point over the Beresina, and on 28 November took up position on the hills above Studienka.

The Russian General Wittgenstein advanced against them, captured Partonneaux's 12th Division in a night clash and also captured most of the 2nd Chevau-légers Lanciers of Berg who were with him. Their standard was also captured.

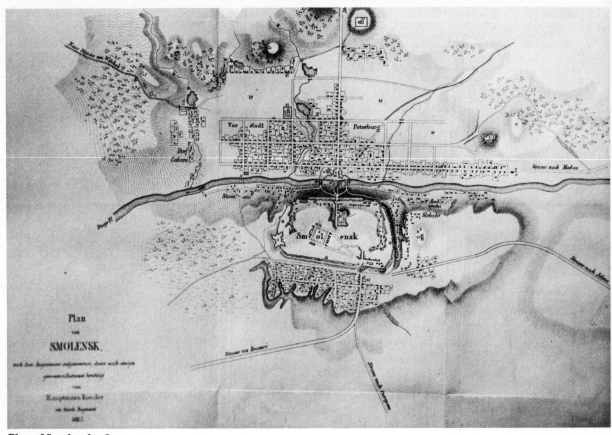

Plan of Smolensk, 1812

Two troops of the regiment escaped this disaster, as they were on duty in Victor's headquarters. Meanwhile, at Studienka, Victor was holding off Wittgenstein and the Berg infantry was destroyed in this bitter, five-hour battle. Generals Damas and Gauthier were wounded, and that night the brigade consisted of Oberst Genty and sixty armed men. Marshal Victor and Generals Gerard and Fournier were also wounded, and the command of IX Corps passed to Markgraf Wilhelm of Baden. The Berg troops attached themselves to the Baden Brigade, and that night withdrew westwards over the Beresina.

On 2 December IX Corps (as rearguard) clashed again with the Russians at Pleszenitzi and the tiny remnants of the Berg brigade disappeared during the fighting. Only individual stragglers now staggered westwards towards Prussia and safety.

The town of Marienwerder was allocated as rendezvous for IX Corps and 200 infantrymen and 130 dismounted cavalry were concentrated there

in January 1813. On 1 March 1813 the contingent, further reduced by sickness, re-entered Düsseldorf.

The infantry was reorganized into a single regiment and sent to Cherbourg. Later a second regiment was raised. The cavalry formed a single regiment.

The Chevau-légers Lanciers took the field again in 1813, and on 15 August Oberst von Toll was in command of the regiment when it was ambushed at Possendorf and nearly destroyed. The survivors were at Leipzig (16–18 October 1813) with Poniatowski's Corps, and this was the end of their career in the service of the French Emperor. In April 1814 Berg became a Prussian province, and the two infantry regiments became the 28th and 29th Prussian Infantry Regiments. The cavalry became the 11th Prussian Hussars and the 2nd Squadron was sent to Prussia to form part of the new 5th Ulanen-Regiment.

The Regiment Westfalen

It was Napoleon's policy to leave no enemy armed forces behind his lines in lands which he had conquered. Not only did he disband the armies he defeated, he sought to raise new troops from them which were then incorporated into his own armies. One such formation is the little-known Regiment 'Westfalen'.

Napoleon decreed the formation of this regiment at his headquarters in Posen on 11 December 1806 with an order which began – 'In consideration of the fact that the areas on the other side of the Elbe should no longer return to Prussian control and that numerous soldiers are available who wish to pursue the honourable profession of arms, we have decided to assist them in their desire.'

The recruits for the Regiment 'Westfalen' were to be drawn from the discharged Prussian soldiers resident in the areas of Münster, Minden and Erfurt (no mention is made of the men of Eichsfeld who were also brought into the regiment) and also former Brunswick and Oranien-Fulda soldiers. The regiment was to have four battalions, each based on one of the areas mentioned above: General Loison was responsible for recruitment in Munster; General Gobert in Minden; General Bisson in Brunswick; and General Thiebault in Fulda and Erfurt.

Each battalion was to have six companies (probably one grenadier, four fusiliers and one voltigeur) each with 3 officers and 140 men; the regimental total (without officers) was thus 3,360 men. Uniform, headgear, etc., was to be of Prussian pattern so as to make best use of the stocks in the captured magazines and of the material captured at Jena.

Very little material has survived to confirm the formation and career of this regiment. There is, however, a diary of a former N.C.O. of the 4th Battalion who later became a Premierleutnant in Kürhessian (Hesse-Cassel) service. This was a man called Vogler. Fieffe, in his *History of the Germans in the Service of France*, and Thiebault in his *Memoirs*, give us also slight hints as to their battle history, uniform and formation.

Thiebault's 4th Battalion was formed of three companies of Oranien-Fulda soldiers and three companies of soldiers from Erfurt. The soldiers from Oranien-Fulda came partially from the Fürstbischoflich-Fulda Upper Rhine Kreisregiment, from the Prussian regiment 'Graf Wartensleben' No. 59 which had been garrisoned in Erfurt, and also from the Kurmainz Infantry Regiment 'Knorr'. Thiebault hurried to his task and soon laid samples of his chosen uniform before the commanders of the other battalions so that they were forced to clothe their men as his were. The 4th Battalion thus received the nickname 'le bataillon modele'. Thiebault, however, perverted Napoleon's order concerning the uniform in that instead of blue (Prussian) coats he dressed his men in white (Saxon?) coats with red collars and cuffs.

The flags of the regiment were of the usual Napoleonic pattern for foreign regiments and of the 1805 pattern. In the centre was a white lozenge and each corner of the square cloth was

Lieutenant-General Wittgenstein, one of Napoleon's Russian adversaries in 1812

red or blue as follows: top staff corner, blue; top fly corner, red; bottom staff corner, red; bottom fly corner, blue. In each of the corners was a golden laurel wreath. In gold on the central white field were the words 'L'EMPEREUR DES FRANÇAIS AU REGIMENT DE WESTPHALIE', and on the reverse was 'VALEUR ET DISCIPLINE 4me BATAILLON'.

In April 1807 the 4th Battalion concentrated in Fulda, and on the 15th of the month they marched out under command of Bataillonschef Schenk and reached Burtscheid (now part of Aachen) after a march of three and a half weeks via Steinan, Gelnhausen, Hanan, Frankfurt am Main, Mainz, Bingen, Bacharach, Boppard, Koblenz, Andernach, Remagen and Jülich. Here it joined the rest of the regiment, which now was commanded by Oberst Erbprinz von Hohenzollern-Sigmaringen.

On 20 May 1807 the regiment marched out via Maastricht, Tongern, Louvain, Brussels, Ath.

Tournai, Lille, Bailleul and Montcassel to St Omer which they reached on 3 June. After a short rest they continued to Calais which they reached on 10 June. By this time so many men had deserted that the four battalions of the regiment had to be reduced to two.

Here the regiment was issued with new muskets and then marched via Grevelingen, Dunkirk, Nieuport, Bruges, Ghent, St Nicolas and Antwerp to Mecheln, which it reached on 25 June and where it remained as garrison. During this period of static duty the time was spent concentrating the capable men into the 1st Battalion and the less capable men into the 2nd Battalion. On 1 November 1807 the 1st Battalion marched off to Spain under Schenk's command, where on 4 January 1809 it was completely absorbed into the French Army. During 1809 its strength was so reduced that it was combined with the Hanoverian

Plan of the area of the Beresina crossing, 1812

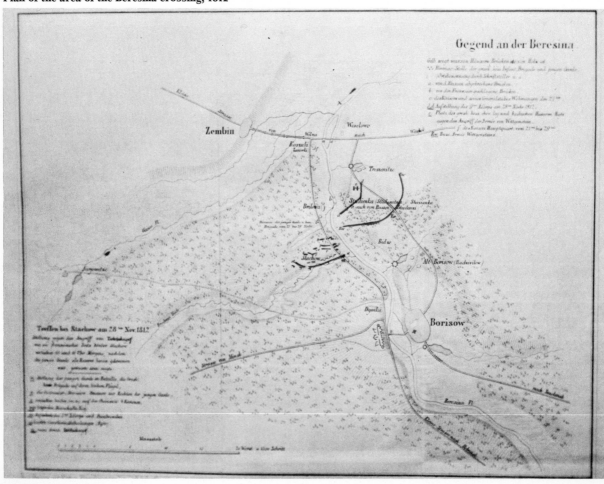

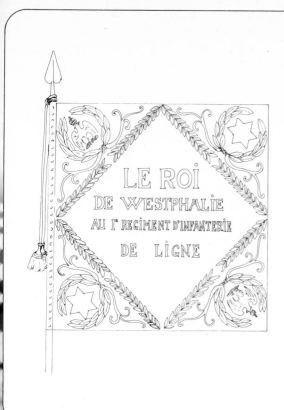

Westfalian 1808-pattern flag

Westfalian button designs, left to right: Grenadier-Garde, Füsilier-Garde, Jäger-Garde and Garde du Corps: Kürassiers 1808–12 and line infantry 1807–13: Kürassiers 1812–13

Legion, which in its turn was disbanded on 9 August 1811.

The 2nd Battalion of the regiment left Mecheln on 4 January 1808 under command of the Erbprinz von Hohenzollern-Hechingen, and marched to Kassel which it reached on 29 January. Here the officers and men were used to re-establish the 2nd Westfalian Line Infantry Regiment which was destroyed at Leipzig in 1813.

SOURCES

Gerdes, A., *Die Geschichte der Truppen Berg und Westfalen 1812 in Russland*

Knötel, *Handbuch der Uniformkunde*

Lossberg, *Briefe in die Heimat*

Lunsmann, F., *Die Westfälische Armee*

Olmes, J., *Heere der Vergangenheit*. Tafeln

Oman, C., *History of the Peninsular War*

Zeitschrift für Heerestunde

Overkott, F., *In Russland Vermisste aus Rheinland und Westfalen*

Thomas, *Un Regiment Rhenan sous Napoleon Premier*

SEE ALSO: von Pivka, *King's German Legion* and *The Black Brunswickers*, both published in 1973 by Osprey Publishing

EXHIBITS: Braunschweigische Landesmuseum; Museum für deutsche Geschichtes – East Berlin

DOCUMENTS: Archiv der Stadt Krefeld; Landeshauptarchiv Düsseldorf; The Lipperheide Costume Collection – West Berlin; The Hewig Collection (now in possession of Dr Kleitmann, West Berlin)

The Plates

GRAND DUCHY OF KLEVE-BERG

A1 Fusilier, 1st Infantry Regiment, 1807–8

Like those of many of Napoleon's satellite states, the infantry of the grand duchy wore white uniforms, this being the Emperor's favourite colour. (In 1806 he even launched a scheme to clothe the French line infantry in white, but this was never completely introduced and was soon abandoned.) Badges of rank were after the French style, and were worn on the lower sleeves by N.C.O.s: one diagonal stripe in facing colour for corporals, one gold stripe edged in facing colour for sergeants. *Fouriers* (company quartermasters) wore corporal's rank badges and a gold stripe edged with facing on the upper arms, and sergeant-majors two gold stripes edged in facing. The rank was also indicated on the shako top band (one gold stripe for sergeants, two for sergeant-majors), the shako cords (*raquets* gold and light blue for sergeants, *raquets* and cords gold and light blue for sergeant-majors) and the sabre knots (grenadier privates red, voltigeur privates green, fusilier privates light blue, N.C.O.s with gold mixture according to rank). Within a few months of the formation of the grand duchy the existing weapons of Bavarian and Nassau origin were exchanged for the usual French items including the 1777 musket and the *sabre-briquet*. Initially shako plates and pouch plates bore the crowned 'J' cipher of Joachim Murat, but when that adventurer moved on to the throne of the kingdom of Naples the design changed to the lion of Berg – almost identical to the current badge of the city of Düsseldorf – and later rhombic plates bearing an eagle were also issued.

A2 Drummer of grenadiers, 2nd Infantry Regiment, 1807

It would appear that drummers initially wore the uniform shown here, which is slightly at variance with the usual style of the era, which dictated that drummers wore the reversed colours of their regiment – for example, in this case a light blue coat with white facings would be conventional. This can probably be explained by the fact that the old uniforms of the Bavarian Infantry Regiment 'Kinkel' No. 12 would have been worn until used up, as an economy measure, before the issue of light blue and white uniforms in 1809–13. Further hallmarks of the musician are the white chevrons with a red 'worm' on the sleeves, the edging to the collar and the shako top band. Grenadier items are the red epaulettes, shako cords and plume. The drum is of brass, the apron of white buckskin.

A3 Sergeant-major colour-bearer, 1st Infantry Regiment, 1808

Although a fusilier, this N.C.O. wears fringed epaulettes in light blue with a gold crescent to mark his special status. Fusiliers normally wore white trident-ended shoulder-straps edged in facing colour. The gold stripes on the upper left arm are service stripes, the forearm badges are rank insignia. The shako is the normal French pattern, and the oval plate now bears the rampant lion of Berg, as does the belt plate. The new-pattern, more elaborate cuff of the 1st Regiment is shown here. The 2nd Regiment wore pointed cuffs – see A2 – and the 3rd wore similar cuffs to the 1st, except that the trident-shaped flaps were light blue with white piping and the buttons were white. The 4th Regiment had square light blue cuffs as originally worn by the 1st Regiment.

B1 Chevau-légers Lancier, campaign dress, 1812–13

As in most other armies of the day, the lancer regiments wore the square-topped Polish czapka in deference to the land which gave birth to that particular branch of the cavalry. On campaign the pink-topped czapka was covered with black oilskin but the squadron pompon was apparently still worn. This man is a front-rank soldier and thus carries a lance; second-rank men carried carbines instead. The grey, buttoned overalls with pink side-stripes would be replaced by dark green breeches and hussar-style boots for parade wear. Harness was light cavalry style, as was the horse furniture. It was customary for trumpeters to ride greys, while the rest of the unit rode blacks, chestnuts and bays depending upon supply.

Standard, 1st and 2nd Westfalian Hussars, 1807–13: the
colours of the central crest are as follows: Top left: white
horse on red. Top right: first, two gold leopards on white;
second and fourth, two silver stars on blue over black; third,
gold lion on red; central shield blue with red-and-white-
striped Hessian lion. Centre: gold eagle on blue. Bottom left:
black lion on gold with gold and red rays. Bottom right: first,
two gold lions on red; second, blue lion on white; third, gold
lion on red; fourth, blue lion on gold scattered with red
hearts

Berg Infantry flag, 1809–13

1808 – 1813.

R. Knötel.

**Soldiers of the Kingdom of Westfalia. From left to right:
Garde-Grenadier, Garde-Jäger, Linien-Infanterie, Offizier
der leichten Infantrie, Garde du Corps, Garde-Chevau-légers,
Kürassier, Hussar, Artillerie-Offizier**

*B2 Chevau-légers Lancier, Compagnie d'Élite, full dress,
1812*

It was customary in the French Napoleonic Army
for the first squadron of a cavalry regiment to
contain the 'Elite Company' – or *Leib-Eskadron*, as
the Germans would term it. Berg, being a French
satellite, also adopted this custom. The Compagnie
d'Élite was distinguished by the large black col-
back or busby, and the red epaulettes. Other
companies wore czapkas and plain green shoulder-
straps edged in red. The whole regiment wore
moustaches. The jacket was the traditional
lancer style with piping in the facing colour along
the rear seams of the body and the sleeves.

*B3 Lieutenant, 2nd Infantry Regiment, campaign dress,
1808–13*

Officers' ranks were indicated by gold epaulettes
after the French fashion, and by gold lace trim
at the top, bottom and sides of the shako. Majors
and above wore cocked hats with gold edging,
loop and button, and gold cords. For parades
gold shako cords and (for grenadiers and fusiliers)

suitable plumes would also have been worn. The
sword knot was gold, the gorget silver with the
arms of the grand duchy in gold. Hessian boots
with gold top trim were worn, and the skirts of the
coat were knee-length instead of short, as in the
ranks. The single-breasted spencer was of French
style, and the grey greatcoat was rolled and worn
en bandolier.

C Chevau-légers, full dress, 1807

To those who are familiar with the French
Napoleonic cavalry, the costume illustrated will
appear very similar to that worn by other of its
lancer regiments. Like the title of the regiment,
the uniform underwent many changes before 1813.

THE KINGDOM OF WESTFALIA

D1 Trumpeter, Garde du Corps, 1812

The trumpeter's costume differed from that of the
other soldiers in the following manner: white
helmet crest instead of black, red plume instead of
white, red jacket instead of white, dark blue

Kingdom of Westfalia 1810, Lieutenant-Colonel of the Garde du Corps in full dress

facings instead of red. Trumpeters rode greys; harness was heavy cavalry pattern, and the horses were about one hand higher than those of the light cavalry units.

D2 Grenadier of the Grenadier-Garde, review order, 1812

The French influence in this uniform is, of course, unmistakable; the bearskin, red cords, plume, epaulettes and sword knot were all after the French pattern. Guard status was indicated by the yellow lace on collar, lapels and cuffs and by the length of the coat tails, which for other ranks of the line were very short. The white summer-wear gaiters were replaced by black ones in winter; on campaign loose white or grey trousers were worn over short gaiters and shoes. The calf- or horse-hide knapsack was in general use by continental armies of the day.

Kingdom of Westfalia 1810, Captain-General of the Guard in levée dress

D3 Jäger of the Jäger-Garde, review order, 1812

In accordance with its function as a *jäger* unit — equivalent to *chasseurs* or Rifles — the Jäger-Garde wore dark green uniform, and Guard status was indicated by white lace decoration to collar, cuffs and lapels. The shako plate was a white Westfalian eagle, almost identical to the French eagle in design. Although a *jäger* unit, the great majority used smoothbore muskets as shown here, and rifles were only issued to selected sharpshooters.

E1 Driver, Military Train, 1812

This man's bandoliers and sabre mark him out as belonging to the Horse Artillery; the red facing colour is somewhat unusual, as most Train regiments of the day had light blue facings.

E2 Officer, 1st Hussars, 1812

The two Westfalian Line Hussar regiments were dressed completely in French hussar fashion: ranks were shown by silver chevrons above the cuffs, silver on the shako and silver decoration on the thighs. The original hussar units were raised from Hungarians and thus their uniform is an elaboration of Hungarian national costume. Once again, the Compagnie d'Élite would have worn busbies, and the trumpeters reversed colours. On 23 August 1813 both these regiments went over to the Allies near Zittau, and became the cavalry of the Austrian-German Legion.

E3 Trumpeter, 2nd Hussars, 1812

This man wears the reversed colours of his regiment; that is to say, the rest of the 2nd Hussars wore black French shakos, red plume, pompon according to squadron, white cords, white eagle plate; sky-blue dolman, pelisse and breeches, with white lace and buttons and black fur trim. The barrel sash was red and white.

F1 Officer of grenadiers, line infantry, campaign dress, 1812

By 1812 all Westfalian line infantry regiments wore the same dark blue facings and yellow buttons, and were differentiated only by the number raised on the flat button. The gold gorget bore the silver Westfalian eagle. As a grenadier officer this man wears a red plume; voltigeurs wore green plumes with yellow tips, and fusilier officers pompons in the company colours.

Kingdom of Westfalia 1810, Chasseur-Carabinier

solution of Westfalia in 1813. The uniform was as for the line infantry except that the buttons were white and the collar, cuff-flaps and lapels were decorated with white lace. The French-style shako plate was rhombic, of white metal, bearing a Westfalian eagle with a shield on the breast charged with the cipher 'JN'. Grenadier rankers wore red epaulettes, plumes and cords; voltigeurs, green and füsiliers, dark blue epaulettes, with white shako cords and pompons in the company colour.

G1 Trooper, Chevau-légers Garde, 1812

The black helmet was of boiled leather and the gilt trim included a frontal shield bearing the 'JN' cipher. The usual Guards distinctions were worn, i.e. lace decoration (in yellow in this case) to collar, chest and cuffs. Only the front-rank men of the regiment carried the lance, and they also carried pistols clipped to the bandoliers on which second-rank men carried their carbines. Saddle furniture was a dark green shabrack with broad yellow edging and the crowned cipher 'JN' in the pointed rear corners. The portmanteau was round, dark green, with red piping at the ends and a yellow circle in the centre of each end-piece. The light-cavalry-style harness was black with brass buckles.

F2 Officer of light infantry, 1812

When first raised the light infantry battalions wore a light blue uniform with orange facings, but this combination of colours was rather too strong and was soon abandoned in favour of the dark green with light blue facings illustrated here. All uniform articles were very similar to the French pattern of the day, and the tactical employment of these light troops was entirely according to French military doctrine, whereby they fanned out ahead of assault columns of the line and kept up a punishing individual fire at the rigid enemy ranks until the columns were close enough to charge them.

F3 Officer of grenadiers, Infantry Regiment 'Königin', 1812

Raised in 1812, this regiment had but a short existence before being swallowed up in the dis-

G2 Officer, 1st Kürassiers, 1808

When first raised in 1808 this regiment had no kürasses; they received them in 1811, and changed their uniform at that time, from that illustrated here to dark blue with crimson facings and yellow buttons. The kürass was of the French pattern, steel with brass rivets and shoulder-chains; the heavy, straight swords (*pallasches*) were also French in design. On campaign it was common for the heavy jackboots to be left in store, and instead the men wore grey buttoned overalls and short boots with screw-in spurs. Saddle furniture was a dark blue, square shabrack edged in the facing colour, and a square dark blue portmanteau with a similar edging. The heavy cavalry harness was black with brass buckles. The 2nd Kürassiers wore blue coats with orange facings and yellow buttons.

Lancer, Cleve-Berg Regiment

G3 Corporal of voltigeurs, line infanry, 1812
This soldier is in review order – that is, ready to be inspected by a general or even by the Emperor himself, who might quite possibly tell him to unpack his knapsack to ensure that it contained the regulation items. Reviews frequently took place while on campaign and were used by commanders to determine the condition and combat fitness of their army. The rhombic shako plate bears the Westfalian eagle with a shield on the breast charged with the 'JN' cipher, and the regimental number cut through the brass below it so that the number shows up black.

H1 Gunner, Horse Artillery of the Guard, 1812
The uniform shown here is rather similar to that worn by the equivalent French unit, except that the Westfalians wore shakos and the French bulky colbacks. The red lace at collar and lapel indicates Guard status. The rhombic brass shako plate bears crossed cannons under a crown; the red 'Hungarian' thigh knots indicate the light cavalry nature of the Horse Artillery.

H2 Officer, Foot Artillery, 1812
Once again the French influence is unmistakable, with the dark blue uniform picked out with red facings and yellow buttons. The shako plate bears crowned crossed cannons, and the silver Westfalian eagle decorates the gold gorget.

H3 Trooper, Hussars 'Jerome Napoleon', 1813
The popular rumour has it that Napoleon gave his brother Jerome 'a regiment of hussars' as a present in 1813. What Jerome in fact received was a collection of half-trained French conscripts without horses or harness (where would Napoleon have found horses to give away in 1813?) and some without uniforms. The flamboyant red shakos and dolmans of the regiment soon earned them the nickname *Die Krebse* – 'The Lobsters' – from the people of Kassel. Trumpeters wore the same shako as illustrated here, but white dolman and pelisse and red breeches.